I0114775

William Mile

IMAGINE

Toward A
BROTHERHOOD
OF MAN

AR
PRESS

Paperback ISBN: 978-1-966283-95-9
Hardcover ISBN: 978-1-966283-96-6

1. Main category—Religion & Spirituality › New Age › New Thought
2. Other category—Nonfiction › Politics & Social Sciences › Social Sciences › Sociology › Social Theory
3. Other category—Nonfiction › Politics & Social Sciences › Philosophy › Good & Evil

AR
PRESS

Published by: American Real Publishing
Roger L. Brooks, Publisher
roger@americanrealpublishing.com
americanrealpublishing.com

TABLE OF CONTENTS

"Do you really think this is as good as we can be as a nation? I don't think the vast majority of people think that. There are probably anywhere from 10 to15 percent of people out there that are just not very good people, but that's not who we are.

"The vast majority of the people are decent, and we have to appeal to that, we have to unite people—bring them together, bring them together."

—President Joe Biden

INTRODUCTION

Throughout history, man has been plagued by two things: evil and the problem of how to lessen it or make it more bearable. In order to remedy evil, we must understand it and its source. For thousands of years, we have failed at this.

In *Imagine: Toward a Brotherhood of Man*, I offer an understanding of evil and its source, as well as a potential remedy. My solution might not be perfect, but it's far better than anything formulated for solving this problem in the past.

With a better understanding of the source and profile of evil, you can conduct the business of living more smoothly. This book will be your guide for surviving and thriving in a world where good and evil coexist. You'll gain a firm mastery over the topic, enabling you to excel in day-to-day affairs and conduct business transactions more efficiently. It's meant to be read, studied, and quite easily understood so you can put its wisdom into practice and move on with your life.

If you have ever wanted purpose in your life and to feel like you belonged—if you've ever wondered why things seem so off and how things could possibly get better again—then this is the right book for you.

An intelligent man once said, "The working state is the highest state." I tend to agree with that statement in spite of the fact that today, finding people who are willing to work to find their true passion is difficult. Fortunately, this book remedies that situation too! Once you've read about the 8:2 theory described within these pages, you'll realize the same thing that intelligent man said!

That's why I wrote this book—to help you turn things around. I want your life to run smoother, easier, so that you can find fulfillment and happiness on a daily basis. Congratulations on embarking on this journey!

Good luck,

William Mile

CHAPTER 1

8:2

Think back to your experiences in school while growing up. Maybe you got along with most everyone, but in every class there were probably a handful of kids who simply weren't very good people. I'm betting that out of thirty students about six of them were troublemakers; kids who weren't really there to learn, nor to belong to a community that desired to.

8:2 theory refers to two things. Out of 10 humans, 8 are brothers tied together by the love God has for them, along with his transformative power that he uses to improve them and their situation. They are as brothers from another mother—united regardless of religious affiliation, race, ethnicity, gender, age group (children and young adults included), or anything else. Given an opportunity to learn this new knowledge, the 8s will be able to work on creating a society with limitless cultural potential. The 8s might not be aware they are actually brothers, nor that a strong force in the world (let's call him/it God) deeply loves them. But the truth is that God wants all of us to survive and thrive—or *surthrive*—as 8s. The problem is the remaining 2, whom God deeply loves also but whose hearts/minds are extremely difficult to reach. Let's just say they're born with innate behavioral habits that equate to them being anything but your brother—and they're certainly not 8s!

The 2s are subtly powerful enough to dupe most of the 8s into being and feeling divided. The reason all this is new to you is because for thousands of years, the 2s have done a heck of a job deceiving the planet. The 8s, whether Christian, Jewish, Muslim, or whatever, have lived in stupor for a very long time.

But how have 2s been able to accomplish all this? And why haven't the 8s caught on until now? For one, the 2s use weird powers from evil sources they are born with to blind, trick, and confuse 8s. 2s are extremely cunning—indeed, they have been behind most of humanity's suffering, and they won't ever stop.

That is, until the 8s do something to stop them. When enough 8s understand what this book is saying, the plans of the 2s could be halted. We 8s just have to be determined to drive our lives in another direction.

The 2s are unlike the 8s in that they hunger after material gains and will stop at nothing to attain their desires. Their subtle powers are so mesmerizing and seductive that they are usually successful at achieving their goals. Until now that is, for when we're armed with this knowledge of 8:2, things can turn around. A powerful idea to keep in mind is that becoming a strong 8 keeps the plans of the evil 2s at bay. Don't worry about other 8s, at some point, 8:2 theory might become so popular all anyone will need to know about it is this book, so we don't need to be concerned about whether other 8s are doing their job; just do yours.

It's reasonable to ask how 8s can be brothers united by god's love and transformative power when things seem to be so wrong in the world. Yes, it's true life seems gloomy at times, almost unreal. But the theory still holds, it's only that the reality of it has been hidden from us, thus disallowing true sustainable change to exist. The fact that for most of our history as people we've been unaware of 8:2 theory shows just how sinister and powerful 2s are. If we are in doubt, fighting among ourselves, confused, and in despair, 2s are thrilled. Their main desire in life is material wealth and to be admired. It doesn't matter what it takes to accomplish their goals.

8:2 theory doesn't promise heaven on earth. There are no promises with 8:2 theory. It's about possibilities, and for opportunities and good scenarios to come about. Sufficient people must not only know about it- but firmly grasp it as well. If there's anything we've learned from reading about 8:2 theory it's that there's a lot of work ahead, but having the necessary purpose and belonging will make it doable. It's an endless endeavor that requires the commitment, willpower, and strength to continue pursuing the goal.

Wrapping up, 8:2 theory explains how out of every 10 humans, 8 are brothers united by the love of God and his transformative power he uses to improve their situation. The remaining 2 are difficult for God to reach and desire only chaos and mayhem for the planet. A great way to get acquainted with 8:2 theory is by analyzing some historical moments and pointing out exactly what we've been discussing.

CHAPTER 2

THE STORY

For as far back as civilization goes, the evil 2s have been methodically at work achieving their desired fate for humanity. In some cases—for example World War II, when people were exterminated because of their race by the millions in very sinister ways—2s got close to achieving their ultimate goals. However, great men of leadership stood up to this evil and stopped their plans from going further.

The evil duo—let's call them "evil people with successful actions"—operate from a completely different source than the 8s, which is a big reason why God has such a difficult time reaching them with his love and transformative power. The duo's source operates from an energy that opposes the 8s, and they want nothing to do with God's love or power. While God is constantly trying to bring the duo of 2s back into brotherhood with the 8s, many nevertheless remain 2s all their lives, staying in a state of corruption that opposes anything good from ever evolving on this planet.

One of the biggest problems the 8s face is that the 2s aren't called "evil people with successful actions" for no good reason. The sinister duo is extremely accomplished at using their ungodly and subtle powers to create havoc in the world. As you can plainly see by studying history, or just watching the news, the 8s haven't been able to get a break. The duo's strategy seems to be to divide the 8s and sow seeds of distrust and contempt between them, so that the 8s end up believing every man on this planet is his rival. Christians, Jews, Muslims, Hindus, all are constantly bickering about who the true god really is and whom he loves most. They don't understand the 2s are involved heavily in fostering this discord, so they fight among each other while the sinister duo waits and creates opportunities to finally have their WWII moment again. It's almost unreal that the 8s, as smart and beloved by God as we are, have missed a really important truth about this world—the problem is not so much with the majority of 8s but with the sinister evil 2s using their powers to confound us.

However small the problem of the 2s seems, however insignificant, the truth remains that throughout history, they have been extremely successful at creating a mess of humanity. If you learn one lesson from this 8:2 theory of good and evil, it's to know your enemy and look out for yourself. The 2s are extremely powerful, and they desire nothing but your downfall; they will laugh and revel in it. If there's a second lesson 8s need to learn, it's to realize that other 8s are not your real problem: only the 2s are. Once you know this, you can surthrive by focusing on you and your goals without all the confusion.

Remember, 8s are brothers. No matter their gender, religion, age group, or social status, they are family because of their openness to a good source we'll call God. Along with their faith, science and the problem-solving mind are the biggest allies of the 8s. Left to their own devices, the 8s are loved by God and quite easily transformed by his power to become the best version of themselves. It's the evil 2s who create doubts in 8s, causing them to fight among each other and seemingly get nowhere.

As you already know, 8s come from all backgrounds—they can be children or adults, men or women, rich or poor. The evil people with successful actions also come from all walks of life. They're not just rich dumb people who want to control the world (these are also possible 2s, though they could just be very scared and confused 8s). Evil 2s can be your teachers, neighbors, parents, siblings, crossing guards—any and every walk of life is a possible position for a 2. They can also be young and old, a college graduate or a dropout. Remember, they're successful because they're able to catch 8s off guard. They wait for just the right moment to use their powers and take full advantage.

The 8:2 knowledge is new to you because for so long the 2s have been able to control our perceptions of what is reality, what is right or wrong, what is worth living for, etc. They've led humanity down dark paths in an attempt to fulfill their goals of WWII-like chaos. Then, when they're handed full control of the situation, they can further reduce humankind to a ghost of what we really are: a brotherhood loved deeply by God.

A few more important things to know about 8s. We too are capable of doing similar "evil" things as 2s, but the difference is that, instead of being led to do them by dark, powerful, evil forces, 8s tend to enact these evils out of ignorance and confusion. Other times, 8s get into trouble because they live by a code that says the acts are warranted in order for the greater good to prevail, as with Robin Hood, for example. Lastly, evil acts can be a result of a simple mistake, an err in the logical mind that causes an 8 to commit actions they will later regret.

On the other hand, when the evil duo with successful actions commit sinister acts, they laugh about it. There's no doubt of their intentions. They never believe they're at fault, and if they apologize, they're lying. That's another thing—in order to get what they want, 2s lie about everything, using their powers of evil to make 8s believe.

If the evil people of successful actions seem unstoppable, that is because knowledge like this has rarely been presented to halt their plans from ever happening. The 8s have been fighting with each other for so long, not realizing they are fighting the wrong enemy. The power of this 8:2 theory is limitless in its scope and has the potential to change every aspect for the better. God's love and transformative power are the most important things uniting 8s. Combine that love with hard work and respect for the scientific method, and we could create a world where people could live, love, learn, work, and play without the hurdles of confusion and chaos 2s have created.

Let's go ahead and give an overview of the ranks of humans within the 8s. First off, these ranks aren't meant to divide us but to help us understand so we are clear about our own path—there is always some form of seniority in life. Within the 8s, there is a small group of leaders at the top of the evolutionary scale. These are usually the best of the best in their chosen vocations, though this is not always the case. They are often the most evolved 8s, able to lead well and approach life with grace. They're the least in numbers because the best usually are; if they weren't, everyone would be the best. The next group are like the second-place finishers. They are good at dealing with life and can sometimes be good leaders too. Lastly is the third group, belonging to a class of humans who struggle a lot in life. Members of this third group must go through many challenges before they can realize they can evolve to become like the second group in the brotherhood of 8s—the 2nd place finishers. However, even when the third group's awareness grows, their history of challenging experiences remains.

Finally, there's the fourth group of humans. They are the last of the 8s, hard workers and good at following directions. Sometimes they follow the wrong directions because they are confounded by the 2s powers, or they just plain make mistakes. These are the ranks of the 8s, roughly speaking. With the knowledge of 8:2 theory and all of its nuances, it's possible that all 8s are able to rise above their obstacles and create something better than anything they've ever thought possible. When they become aware of the real problem and stop bickering among each other, a future worth living becomes possible.

Let's once more be clear, however, that a lot of work lies ahead. Fortunately, understanding the 8:2 theory allows this work to be much more seamless. In other words, the 8:2 theory makes working toward a livable future more doable. If the 8s are too lax in their efforts, the 2s evil people with successful actions will once more wreak havoc on the population.

CHAPTER 3

ON GOOD AND EVIL

Throughout history, the evil people of successful actions have effectively spread lies and half-truths about many topics, and for humanity to evolve into something better, it's crucial that we perceive these matters clearly. When we're awash in the lies, it's difficult to grow, to progress. The evil 2s have had great success in their ability to sow seeds of doubt and discord among the 8s, never allowing us to fully live up to our potential.

The question of whether we are good or bad is one such topic the evil 2s have successfully distorted, serving only to further confuse the 8s. Without a clear answer, how will the 8s advance?

The topic of whether people are good or bad has three groups contending against each other for the right to be right. One group says people are all born good but suffering and bad situations turn them bad. Another says we're all born bad and need discipline to learn how to act correctly. And a third less popular group states we're neither good nor bad but bring with us good and bad habits from our parents' gene pool, which express themselves (or don't) in this current life.

It seems that regardless of what answers we've come up with, we're not satisfied. The 2s have been successful in never allowing the 8s to believe there's a viable solution to the problem causing their suffering and keeping them from rising above their doubts. The 2s revel in the misery of the 8s, amused at the confusion and suffering we experience. And they are set to keep the confusion going until they have their WWII moment—the population surrendering their wills over to the 2s and allowing them to do whatever they want. The 2s want the 8s to doubt and never feel happy with our lives because it gives them power!

Good and evil exist, and people basically act in good and bad ways for various reasons. But evil done by 2s is different. They commit these heinous acts for fun. They love chaos, and don't care for good or God. They serve disorder and seem to only feel comfortable when things are going bad.

In order to attain their goals, the evil people of successful actions lie about everything and never take any responsibility for their acts. They will deny all wrongdoing like you wouldn't believe. Remarkably, they have been successfully implementing this strategy throughout history in order to rig the whole human drama into a scenario most 8s would rather not live in.

Only 8s can change the quality of their lives. No one is going to do it for them. They only need to step up to the challenge. If we want something different we must do something different, otherwise we get more of the same results we don't want.

8s have the responsibility to never allow 2s to gain control. Equipped with 8:2 theory, 8s have the opportunity to build the world as they themselves envision—a different, better world than the ones the 2s try to force upon them.

While the 8:2 theory offers plenty of possibilities for a better future for humankind, it does so without promising utopia, because that's just not realistic. There is no perfect Earth where pain is gone and everything is blissful and nothing ever goes wrong—that's heaven! If anyone promises you a world without suffering, run the other way quick! But the 8:2 theory promises a future that *is* possible, a world where people can find purpose and meaning in work again. After all, this is Earth! We're here to work. We're makers, doers. We create things, and there is always some work that needs to get done. And instead of it being a dreadful thing, work is actually the only way to fend off the evil 2s. Purpose through work and a sense of belonging to the goal of keeping the 8s in control of the world are the two main attributes of 8:2 theory.

So are we good or bad? Well, imperfect humans do good and bad things, but the 8:2 theory allows us to see the roots of our real problem: the 2s.

CHAPTER 4

THE EVIL 2s

Ever meet or know someone you considered evil? Someone so sickly deranged it was mindboggling how this person had risen to their seat of power and prestige? Let's turn our attention to this evil, examine it, get to know it, so that in this way there is no mystery which gives it any more strength to trick us. Shining a spotlight on evil reveals it, so we can plainly know it when it shows up.

Let's start with their title. By "evil," what do we mean? Do we mean it in some sort of funny way, like a joke? No! Think of the main evil character in the three big monotheistic religions and have him take human form. Most know him as Satan, the evil one that desires harm on all humanity and uses trickery to confound them. That's the kind of evil 8:2 theory refers to, the kind of evil that kills millions of people because of their race or religion. It's the evil that causes wars for the purpose of attaining riches or land, as opposed to wars that set out to defeat real enemies who kill and destroy for thrills. There are countless examples of evil in history—as well as on the daily news—you know it when you see it. Let's review some examples in history of how evil 2s propagated their agendas.

Evil 2s are not only capable but more than willing to accuse 8s of being the real evil in the world. It happened during WWII when one country's dictator accused a whole race and several other groups of being the main problem—and then went on to try to erase them from the population through genocide. It happened slowly yet deliberately. Using their powers of deception, they methodically destroyed any threat to the achievement of their end goal; wealth, name, and power at any cost.

Let's look at another example in history how evil 2s attempted to make their mark.

During the inquisitions in Europe leaders in powerful religious institutions prohibited any talk or writing that went against official Catholic ideas. Going so far as using torture on individuals who wanted to help humanity through science. Anything deemed going against the church's teachings was grounds for this sort of treatment. Evil 2s weren't limited to the role of strict authoritarian religious leaders. They could easily be regular people, our neighbors, who knew individuals in power, and would let them know when they saw anyone in their community "misbehaving."

In certain authoritarian countries around the world, where leaders were basically viewed as infallible icons, or parental figures, it was common practice to round up all intellectuals, scientists, artists, anyone who might be seen as a threat, and have them sent to "reeducation" camps where often they'd never be seen by family or friends again. It was taboo to be smart, to have new ideas, to find better solutions for problems in these authoritarian countries. Evil 2s in this type of scenario many times enjoyed employment as secret police agents, or propaganda pushers, probably even worse, as spies paid by authorities to tell on their own family members.

As we've just seen, 2s are not only evil, but quite successful at being so. Another sad fact you might have discovered through these examples is that some people actually root for the evil 2s. Now, these fans of evil 2s aren't necessarily evil themselves, but we can say they aren't all there, and are one of the challenges 8s will face when working toward creating a different world. 2s are evil yes, they're 8s main problem, but what about the support from some 8s? We need to understand these two factors that work together if we want a different world.

You may ask why God allows for 2s to exist and create such misfortune for the rest of the planet. My honest opinion is it's just the way it is, and it's going to continue until something is done about it. And what 2s have done throughout history should spur 8s to action! Now that we know what we're up against, our fate is in our own hands. We can create a new, better world free from the influence of the 2s, but to do so, we need a strategy.

CHAPTER 5

TIPS FOR 8s

How do we stop the 2s from creating problems and unnecessary drama in the world? How can we start creating a world that resembles what 8s would like to see?

The advice in this chapter stems from my own opinions about the best plan of action 8s can take to avoid the influence of the 2s. I encourage the 8s to analyze this advice using the 8:2 theory as a sort of measuring standard and come up with their own conclusions.

To better our chances at bringing about a world we want instead of a world we've mostly known, the following tips and advice are offered. Firstly, as far as practical actions, masters throughout history have given us many helpful tools to make human life less chaotic. Moses had the 10 commandments. Jesus proclaimed the human elements of faith, hope, and love. Buddha's followers were given the 5 noble truths along with 5-7 precepts for right living. The Koran taught its faithful followers to be disciplined in prayer and fasting.

My list of suggestions for 8s in modern times contains only four parts. You're welcome to use them along with any from your own religion or philosophical background. I tried to choose basic advice that would be best suited for 8s in light of 8:2 theory, though there's room for adjustments.

First, stay away from intoxicants as much as possible. Anything clouding your mind will make it easier for 2s to deceive you. Substances like these tend to warp perceptions and make us more susceptible to negative influences.

For most of sports history mind altering substances were banned. Not only do they reduce performance levels but they can cause all sorts of mental distortions causing players to skip practice, forget meetings, and get into negative moods, which all contribute to a team's demise. As a team of 8s we have to be sober enough to stick to the game plan.

Second, 8s should be motivated to develop themselves physically and mentally to their fullest potential. By fully developing our minds and bodies we'll be better equipped to tackle any and all deceptions evil 2s try to use on us. I encourage 8s to find mentors, read books and articles related to self-improvement, and to apply themselves to implementing the strategies they learn while knowing the work is never finished.

Third, 8s should largely focus on discovering what kind of work they will do to sustain themselves in order to depend less on any assistance, become natural leaders, and a positive force in their circle of influence. By focusing on your work, you can become self reliant, sustain your life, and help others through service.

Lastly, as promised, my fourth suggestion is that you pass on what you've learned to future generations. This way the knowledge doesn't disappear when we leave this planet. Decide on some way to give back to your community, so that future 8s have something they can use to avoid living in a world where evil 2s run the show again. Remember, there are two ways to leave a legacy, write a book worth reading, or live a life worth writing about.

Aside from the practical tips I've just shared, below I'll supply ideas which can also aid in developing a better world. These tips are more mental, or philosophical in nature, but nevertheless just as powerful as the practical ones. Read them and see how they can help clear the air on many things that could arise from getting acquainted with 8:2 theory.

Let's look at some ways 8s can improve their chances at creating a better planet to live in. They are a worldwide brotherhood united by God's love. As such, they're able to tap into God's transformative power and use it to make themselves and their situations better. The biggest takeaway from the 8:2 theory is that 8s should let each other enjoy God the way they want to. Let other 8s worship, praise, and learn about God the best way they know how. Don't meddle in the spiritual business of other 8s unless asked or unless the opportunity opens up organically. Remember that all 8s are our allies and that we are strongest when we work together. When powerful and united, we 8s can reduce the 2s influence over us and create a new world!

The majority of 8s have to learn how to make a living or accomplish goals while trusting two things: their God, with his love and transformative power, and the leadership of the higher, more evolved 8s. They have to trust that these more evolved 8s will do their jobs. This is not to say that the majority of 8s should have no opinion, nor that they should blindly be led by "evolved" 8s. Instead, these 8s should trust their gut and remember that "shit happens," so they should do their darndest to work on themselves and their goals.

Each member of the brotherhood of 8s needs to learn how to formulate their own opinions about things while maintaining a healthy relationship with other 8s. That's not to say we will be best friends with all other 8s, but at least understand there's a deep connection between us and we must allow each other freedom of choice without judgment. We need to commit to becoming smarter, better, faster, and stronger in every way. The health of the planet, your brotherhood, and the future depends on it!

It is believed that the Dark Ages happened in Europe a long time ago and ended a long time ago. The 8:2 theory says it's all been the dark ages until now. Only now, with this 8:2 knowledge, is the transformation of the everlasting dark age of humanity into something better finally possible. I can't quite say what this transformation looks like—it's still a work in progress—but I know it beats anything we've managed to come up with so far. We have a long way to go before this dark age evolves into a reality that's more to the 8s liking—and a lot of willpower and determination will be required to keep this new something going far into the future—but as they say…step by step.

CHAPTER 6

ON GOD

Let's be real—a lot of people believe in God without going to church or adhering to all the rules, and they are fine. Even without attending temple or any holy place of worship, these people maintain a deep faith in something that makes them happy and brings meaning to their lives. It's just a fact that not everyone is meant for church, but they can still love reading and learning about religion. They can still live in an ethical way.

As 8s, we need to be more open to people's different journeys and relationships with God. Some meditate, others pray, others love to praise and sing. Others feel like they are in the presence of something amazing when they're out in nature. We 8s would do well to learn from other 8s—or just leave them alone and be okay with the way they show praise and worship to God. If you have an opinion, remember that strong 8s keep the plans of the evil 2s at bay. Evil 2s love to divide people on the topic of God. They enjoy antagonizing us and instigating religious discord. As a result, even among people of similar faiths, there is a ton of infighting. The evil 2s laugh inside, knowing their plans of world domination inch closer to being real with every argument people have about God and religion. In the end, 2s want complete control over unhappy, miserable people whom they've helped put in that condition. The sad part is that without the 8:2 theory, the 8s will gladly give them that control as long as they're promised something better—or something that *seems* like it.

In general, 8s need to mature. By putting aside silly ideas of whose faith is truer, we can get down to the business of living, raising families, conducting our affairs, and protecting what matters (i.e., everything on this planet) from evil 2s. God is so much more than any one faith can completely describe. Ever wonder why every year hundreds if not thousands of new books and commentaries get released? New ideas about God happen all the time.

I definitely don't pretend to be some expert on the subject. But I do have some experience. God—light, wisdom, something all-powerful and benevolent—brought me out of a very bad situation I was in for many years. Circumstances that not many people would want to be in, ever! Anyway, this book is dedicated to that benevolent being who answered my prayers many years ago.

Believing that we have all the right answers—and that no one else does—is a problem we as 8s need to overcome. I say 8s, not Christians or Jews or any other religion, because people of almost all faiths tend to believe much the same thing. They think only their religion is right, and others need to catch on. It's okay to disagree, to have different beliefs—in fact, it's very healthy—as long as we remember strong 8s keep the plans of the evil 2s at bay.

As long as 8s are clear on this powerful idea, you can have your faith and believe whatever you want. As 8s, we have three things going for us—our faith in something benevolent we call God, our faith in our own ability to solve problems, and our faith that advanced 8s will do their jobs and things will pan out for all of us.

I'll share a little about my own personal faith. For many years I had faith in God…still do. I went to church, got baptized, and learned as much as I could about him and the blessings that accompany a deep faith in him and his promises. However, one day I prayed to be able to overcome a stubborn obstacle that had lasted many years, and the answer I received as a thought or instinct was surprising. God opened me up to knowledge that wasn't primarily from the Christian faith. In fact, he opened me up to knowledge sources from all over the world. I became interested in different books, instructions, meditation, prayers, etc. I said to God, "If this is the path that will remove this stubborn obstacle from my life, so be it! I trust the process. Thank you!"

The point is that at first, I, too, wasn't very open to knowledge that didn't come directly from the holy book, which I was brought up to believe had most of it. However, when my obstacle was as bad as it was, I no longer saw the wisdom in holding on to such beliefs. My prayers were answered, and I became what's known as an educationalist, or someone who studies the ideas of many different subjects broadly in order to come up with my own conclusions. Without my ability to trust in that answer to my prayers, the 8:2 theory would not have been possible.

This 8:2 theory doesn't ask participants of different faiths to change their beliefs. It doesn't ask a Christian to become Hindu, or a Jew to become a Christian, or whatever. What it does call for is a more harmonious existence among ourselves, which means that, when it comes to God, we 8s need to simply let other 8s be. If we keep on fighting among ourselves, it can be expected that the 2s will go on running the show.

Our history as a brotherhood of 8s alongside evil 2s has been pretty bad. Everything on the news is dark and dreary. History books are filled with atrocious events that don't appear to have any end or easing in sight. Things have been and continue to be bad, but trust me, it can get a whole lot worse.

A strong 8 keeps the planet healthy. That's the goal of 8:2 theory, to develop 8s into stronger, smarter, faster, in-dividuals who understand their connection to God, their faith, and their brothers.

This is the reason I keep emphasizing that 8s should let other 8s be no matter how tempting it is to hate or blame. It's an 8s job to trust in God, have faith in themselves, and have faith more advanced 8s will perform their leadership roles adequately so that things pan out.

So, you may ask: *It seems like all we have to do is work hard at creating a world led by 8s and make sure 2s don't take control again. Isn't there anything else?*

I'll answer that with a quote on a sign my grandfather put up on the outer walls of his hardware store:

"Son, work hard. Life is very difficult if we don't."

CHAPTER 7

AN 8:2 FUTURE

Imagine living in a world where no matter what kind of fortune you were dealt, you know that you are an 8 and that other 8s have your back. No matter what adversity you encounter—poverty, sickness, loss, or just the ups and downs of everyday life—you have the mental, emotional fortitude to overcome it all simply because you fully grasp what it means to receive God's love and transformative powers. Imagine how this understanding of belonging to a brotherhood could change things. In a world of new technologies, artificial everything, virtual reality—even augmented reality where reality itself is questioned and people are left feeling bewildered and alone—8s would nevertheless feel a sense of true belonging! That belonging is a strong force capable of creating positive changes that ripple outwards, spreading goodness to countless future generations. Belonging to an elite force like this brotherhood—not to mention having the purpose to keep 8:2 knowledge alive for future generations—is indeed a powerful force. A force that can remove the inertia, burn through the cloudiness, and overcome the negative belief systems that have plagued 8s since the beginning of time.

With this 8:2 knowledge, 8s have been given an opportunity to change things from a world the 2s are happy with, to a world the majority of humankind can be happy with. From an evil minority-controlled world to a world controlled, led, and developed by the best of the majority—a majority that doesn't belong to any one race, religion, sex, age group, or social status, but belongs instead to a brotherhood of 8s from all over the world.

Yes, it will involve work, but you know the saying, "Freedom isn't free." It takes hard work, dedication, and resolve to keep this thing going. No, it won't be without pain. It's not heaven, but it's definitely not hell either. I guess you could call it *earth*—but a better one than we've had thus far! Our purpose of keeping this 8:2 knowledge intact for future generations will keep us busy. Our day-to-day lives will be filled with purpose, so we'll know exactly what's going on, and exactly what's needed. We'll do our jobs, raise our families, and conduct the business of life with more ease. A purpose-driven life is a powerful force for good, but it takes a lot of will as well as desire to keep it going.

The two main benefits of an 8:2 world are purpose and belonging—two powerful forces that will be the foundation of a new world, not to mention the foundation of all our arts, sciences, and day-to-day lives. To get from where we are now to this possibility will require a tremendous push, a herculean effort to free us from the initial state of stupor that the evil 2s have worked so hard to keep us in.

I won't pretend to know all the details, or to even predict that far since revolutions usually take a lot of work. I think it's best to just finish explaining 8:2 theory the best way I can so we have a strong, clear blueprint to work from. My job is to make the 8:2 theory plain enough to make this endeavor possible. The rest is up to us 8s—all of us.

Along with letting other 8s be, thereby creating a strong brotherhood, I think the next best lesson is to develop yourself in every way. Learn as much as you can, even if it's through watching YouTube videos or reading books. Think about all the ways you can become better, smarter, fitter for the long haul. And lastly, keep your faith fresh and strong. God loves you, has big plans for you, wants you to succeed, wants you to have access to the best in life.

If you're asking what you should study, I'd say religion, business, science/technology, medicine/health, and psychology. These are fields that will improve your chances of understanding the world around you while helping you achieve your goals.

CHAPTER 8

8:2 REVIEW AND TAKEAWAYS

To sum up, we've learned about 8:2 theory—the brotherhood of 8 and the evil 2s with successful actions. The principal of 8:2 states that out of 10 humans 8 are a brotherhood in God's family and 2 are not. God wants these 2 to return to the brotherhood, and so he fights to achieve this goal ceaselessly, but it seems a lost cause, and God's love for the 2s goes inevitably unreturned. The theory explains how 8s don't belong to one religion, race, gender, nationality, age group, or any division, but are instead a brotherhood bound by the love of God and his transformative power to change them as well as their situation for the better.

Within the brotherhood of 8s, there are levels of evolution. The top and smallest number of 8s are the best in their fields of work, natural leaders. The next group comes in second place with similar qualities as the first group. The third group really is in the second group but born with a haze over their consciousness that causes them to go through a lot of challenges before realizing this. The remaining 8s are hard workers and usually follow instructions well.

The evil people with successful actions also come from all walks of life—blue collar, white collar, male, female, young, older, short, tall, medium, rich, poor, famous, and whatnot. These 2s are the prime source of confusion among the 8s. With the use of the evil powers they're born with, they are determined to see a future for 8s that includes plenty of misery, death, and suffering.

The key tip for the brotherhood of 8s is that they *can* create a better world by recognizing what they have in common and committing themselves to working together to forge a strong brotherhood. Willing recipients of God's love and transformative power, they belong to an enormous family of 8s!

Q&A

1. Does the 8:2 theory hold that all evil events in the world were caused by evil 2s?

   Great question. I didn't delve into the darkness where the 2s get their powers because we had enough matters to explore without dealing with those evil forces; I decided to keep it simple, because if 8s let other 8s do what they got to do, we'll be okay.

   So I'd say about 90 percent of the world's problems are strongly influenced by the 8s ignorance of 8:2 theory. This ignorance is caused by a couple factors with evil 2s use of super natural powers to keep us in the dark being 1 of them. The other factor being our lack of self-development as humans. We as 8s need to train our minds and bodies to be able to understand 8:2 theory as well as apply it's principals.

The other 10 percent of what causes our events is what great masters throughout history have described as the law of cause and effect; we reap what we sow. We get what we give, or our actions create consequences which we one day will need to face and resolve!

Let's recap what creates our current undesired situation. First, our lack of study and self-development which leads to an ignorance of 8:2 theory. Next, we can choose to blame evil 2s or not as a second factor but don't underestimate their involvement. And lastly the law of cause and effect would be the third contributing factor influencing our current circumstance.

2. What is the ultimate outcome if this theory is adopted by a mass amount of people?

I honestly like to say it's a mystery because it's not up to me, it's up to the 8s! I pray something really good comes about from this book. Of course, not *everyone* needs to come on board. Even though it would benefit 8s to understand and keep this knowledge alive, not all 8s need to adopt the 8:2 theory. Maybe over time that'll change, and it will become the new normal if enough people get it.

All I can say is that life will continue on as it has, only maybe now it'll be just a little smoother. What more is possible after that I really have no idea. But I prefer it that way. I'm a writer—I study stuff and put things on paper. Whatever happens after that isn't up to me.

3. Why write such a weird book? And how did you get the ideas for the theory?

I love weird stuff as long as it functions, is useful, can make people happier, and is somewhat capable of being cool. I think this is why I liked the sci-fi genre as a kid. I read a lot of Stephen King-type books and just loved all things fringe or on the edge of what is and could be. You could definitely catch me watching shows like *Ripley's Believe It or Not* regularly.

The ideas for this theory come from my study of many religious texts and commentaries over the last twenty years. I used to belong to different groups like church, meditation groups, yoga groups, etc. I found that the people there generally liked their "style" of worship or belief system, but me, I wasn't like that at all. I wanted to learn it all and come up with some kind of unifying theory. So that's what I set out to do without knowing exactly how I was going to accomplish this. I meditated on these topics, and my experience along with this knowledge led to the 8:2 theory. I decided to read, read, and read some more. I consulted with clergy, masters, and all kinds of other leaders, but in the end, I was the one who had to do the work of creating a kind of unifying theory out of it all.

If you notice, most religions want you believing in their brand of faith. They don't want to unify—they sort of just want 8s in their group. My theory's a little different, as it seeks to unite all the 8s from all religions, philosophies, etc., and proclaims them to be brothers. My theory also keeps things real by postulating that a minority of 2 out of 10 are evil people of successful actions.

4. How does your first book, *Get Off Your Zen and Get a Job: Work, the Forgotten Spiritual Path*, relate to this current one?

Awesome question! I loved that book. I thought my editor did an amazing job making it more reader-friendly, so I booked him for this project too. It was my first attempt at authoring a book, and by the end of the whole process I was exhausted. In general, I'm happy with it, even though there remain parts of it I'm not thrilled by. There came a time I just wanted it out there and didn't care how many people decided to read it.

Whether or how it relates to this one, I don't know. My first book encouraged people to get to work, and that's what I continued doing in my personal life too. I kept going, and my blog also kept evolving, so I guess I followed my own advice.

As for the content, I'm not sure how they overlap. I do emphasize work in both books. I think it's an important aspect of living. It's probably one of the hardest tasks we're faced with today, finding out what you love and making a living out of it. I think my first book was a stepping stone in the development of

8:2 theory. It's possible that my work as a researcher and passion for discovering reality led to this current work.

5. How is this 8:2 theory superior to other branches of knowledge at helping individuals achieve happiness as well as their set goals?

It's not meant to be better, but it is meant to augment greatly the effectiveness of all preceding knowledges that have been used to help people.

6. What is the danger of a world based on an 8:2 theory where 8s take the lead?

One danger is that we get so good at running the world—and our lives—that we forget why it's running so well. Meaning, we forget the purpose and reason behind this whole thing. If we forget the lessons in history about genocides, for example, and simply replace the existing reality with a world as 8s see it, the danger is that we may become doomed to repeat our past. It's crucial to remember the why of it all in order to not take it for granted. Unfortunately, humans do tend to forget and we love to take things for granted, so it's a real problem.

Another is infighting. If we forget that a strong 8 is what 2s dislike, we'll start to fight again about small things because we slacked off. It's another real problem too, because once that seed of distrust and doubt grows, here come the 2s to capitalize on that. That's when things go back to how they were, and to return from there back to how 8s want it again will be tough.

7. Where can readers who enjoy your book learn more?

I have a blog at www.Williammile.com.

8. Any final thoughts for your readers?

I don't wear robes or study in a monastery for hours a day. I have nothing but respect for those who do, but I felt I had enough information to formulate this 8:2 theory, so I did. I felt that my life-experience and twenty years of sincere practice combined with the study of texts from various religions, including Hinduism, Christianity, Judaism, Islam, Buddhism, etc. were enough to write this book.

Still, I hope you will look to the meaning of the words more so than the words themselves and think for yourself. Use your own brain to figure things out.

This book is an opportunity for the planet to do things more efficiently, to have and create purpose, and to belong to something worthwhile. It's all only possible if 8s see it as such.

I realize that 8:2 theory might be difficult for some people to find applicable. I get it—where is all this information coming from, right? While I honestly don't have *all* the answers, I do believe there are enough answers in this book to make positive planetary change *real*. It does require study, inquiry, and in the final stage, confidence. We need to have faith that what one has discovered for oneself about 8:2 theory will be good.

Lastly, I do believe that as you go through your life with the understanding you've gained from studying 8:2 theory, you will begin to slowly see what matters and what doesn't in your quest to accomplish your goals. Things will become clearer as time progresses, and your dreams and aspirations will become easier to work toward as well as achieve.

Thank you and good luck!

ABOUT THE AUTHOR

As a graduate of William Paterson University in NJ, William earned a Bachelor of Arts degree in Psychology while also propping up a small meditation group on campus in which basic inner spiritual teachings were shared. With over twenty years of meditation experience, as well as having the opportunity to sit with well-known masters, William felt the need to make his own way, abandoning the sitting groups to pursue his curiosities no matter where they led. As he puts it, "There's a freedom achieved only when an individual is true to himself, which can't be found in meditation groups."

You can learn more about his ideas by visiting
williammile.com.